LORD, TEACH US TO PRAY

SIX STUDIES IN SPIRITUALITY AND THE LORD'S PRAYER

LEADER'S GUIDE

John C. Purdy

the KERYGMA
program

Art and Layout: Kathy Boykowycz

Grateful acknowledgement is hereby made for permission to include quotations from the *New Revised Standard Version Bible*, copyright 1989, Division of Christian Education of the National Council of Churches of Christ in the United States of America.

Lord, Teach Us to Pray is published and distributed by The Kerygma Program, Suite 205, 300 Mt. Lebanon Boulevard, Pittsburgh, PA 15234. Phone: 800/537-9462 FAX: 412/344-1823.

ISBN 978-1-882236-03-9

Kerygma on the Web: www.kerygma.com

the KERYGMA
program

Suite 205, 300 Mt. Lebanon Boulevard, Pittsburgh, Pennsylvania 15234

CONTENTS

INTRODUCTION

The Leader

You are most likely reading this *Leader's Guide* because you are considering the possibility of, or have already committed yourself to, leading a group of participants in a creative approach to studying *Lord, Teach Us to Pray*. Whether you are a clergy person, a church educator, or a lay person, it is less important how much you remember about your previous experiences in study groups than that you are now willing to engage in an intensive process of reading, studying, planning, and leading. There are no short cuts to successful leadership of a study group using the Kerygma approach. It will require a significant commitment of time and energy in order to design effective session plans for those who are engaged in this study with you

As a leader of a Kerygma group, you will function in a variety of roles at different times. You are first of all a *learner*. Being a Kerygma leader will provide you with a wonderful opportunity for learning more about the Lord's Prayer. You are not expected to be an expert on all of the material on which the course is based. However, you are expected to be prepared for each session so that you are able to guide the members of the group in a productive study.

As a result of your reading in preparation for leading each session, you will also become a *resource person*. You are not expected to know all the answers to every question that is raised, but you should be able to direct group members to resources that will assist them to find answers for themselves.

Furthermore, you will be a *planner* who works intentionally to consider session plan suggestions, the time available, the needs, interests, and abilities of the participants, and the resources available in order to develop an appropriate plan for each session. The session plans provided in the *Leader's Guide* are very complete and probably offer more than you will be able to accomplish in the time you have. However, the best session plans are ones you construct using the suggestions here as well as your own personal resources and experiences.

Being a *facilitator* of group process is also a very important role for you to perform. The six session plans include many activities that involve participants in investigation, discussion, reflection, creativity, and application. The more comfortable you become in guiding these processes, the more effective the study will be for others. At first, some participants may prefer having you tell them what they should know about the material. And, there will be times when you may be tempted to tell them all that you know. However, you will be most effective as a leader and the group members will gain most from the course when they are guided by you in a variety of participatory activities as you explore the Lord's Prayer together.

Throughout the course of study you will also be called upon to exercise several important qualities. With the constraint of time and the great body of material to explore, you must be *flexible*. Unplanned questions will arise, activities will take longer than anticipated, and participants may want to go more slowly than you feel is necessary. In addition, you will need to be *patient* with the author when the written material is confusing or unclear. And, unpredictable occurrences in the life of the group and the church will require patience.

Those Who Participate in Kerygma Groups

The people who choose to associate with a group that is studying the Bible using Kerygma resources do so for a variety of reasons and bring with them many levels of readiness and ability. When individuals are invited to attend a Kerygma group, they should be made aware from the beginning that this is not a study where the leader does all the work of preparation and presentation. Every participant is expected to have read the Basic Bible References and the appropriate material in the *Resource Book* prior to each session. Familiarity with this material is assumed by the session plans that are developed in the *Leader's Guide*.

Given the busy schedules of most people, there will be times when some come to a session with minimum preparation. You should not compromise the expectation of adequate preparation, because the experience for the whole group will suffer if the reading is not taken seriously. There are several ways you can handle the lack of preparation by participants.

1. Encourage persons who have not read the assignments to delay participation in the discussion until the others have had a chance.

2. Provide some time, as a part of the session plan, to review the key texts that serve as the foundation for the session.

3. When working in pairs or small groups, be sure that those who are not prepared are distributed among the groups rather than being placed together.

Some participants will have had a lot of experience with study groups, but for others this will be the first time they are involved in an in-depth study as adults. It is important for each person to feel that he or she belongs to the group. You will need to encourage both the experienced and inexperienced participants to be mindful and appreciative of each other.

Number of Sessions and Amount of Time

When planning to offer an adult course, it is important to ask and answer several key questions such as: How will this study fit into our adult education program? How many weeks or sessions will we schedule? How much time should be planned for each session? Perhaps these questions have already been answered in your church and the necessary arrangements have been made. If so, you and your group will have to adjust to what is already planned. If the questions have not been answered, you may want to consider a variety of options.

This *Leader's Guide* contains strategies for six sessions. However, there are several ways to adjust the scheduling of those sessions: (a) Six sessions of one hour each can be planned. The materials will work well in this format, but you will have to be selective about which activities to include. (b) You can expand the sessions to 1-1/2 to 2 hours by using more of the activities suggested in the Session Plans. (c) If you are familiar with the material and have additional resources, you might use this course as the basis for building a longer program of study in which you incorporate your own knowledge, expertise, and creativity.

The Printed Resources

A number of printed resources are included as part of *Lord, Teach Us to Pray*. Each resource makes a significant contribution to the whole program.

The Bible

The major curriculum resource for all Kerygma study programs is the Bible. The *New Revised Standard Version* is the translation on which this course is based. However, participants will be able to engage in the study effectively with another translation. In fact, the study will be enhanced by the presence of several translations. A study Bible with notes for each section of the text and other study aids is recommended for the leader as well as the participants. A number of such Bibles are available. Among those containing good study notes are the *New Oxford Annotated Bible with Apocrypha (NRSV)*, *The Oxford Study Bible with Apocrypha*, and the *New Jerusalem Bible (with complete study notes)*.

The *Resource Book*

The *Resource Book* is the text both leaders and participants will use to guide their study. There are usually eight or nine pages of text in each chapter. This volume and the Bible contain all the necessary information to enable persons to participate profitably in the group sessions.

As you review the *Resource Book,* you will note that each chapter begins with a Summary and includes a list of Basic Bible References and a Word List. In the main body of the text, the Basic Bible References are printed in boldface type. At the end of each chapter you will find a section entitled "For Further Study and Reflection." You will want to review this section with the option of directing the group members' attention to it generally or on a week-by-week basis. From time to time this section will encourage participants to use additional study resources. For this purpose the group should have available from the church library several basic reference books, such as a Bible dictionary, commentaries, and some of the volumes listed as supplementary readings for the course.

As a leader, you should read the *Resource Book* from beginning to end before undertaking leadership of a study group and before you start planning any particular sessions. This effort will provide you with an overview of the total course. As you then plan for each session, you will need to reread the appropriate material for this session.

The *Leader's Guide*

This is the book you have in your hands at this moment. It will be the indispensable resource you will use for planning each session. You will notice that each chapter of the *Leader's Guide* contains:

1. "Notes from the Author." Jack Purdy provides background information on the focus of each section. Also included are helpful comments and suggestions for dealing with various aspects of the chapter.

2. "Session Plans." Extensive suggestions for session planning are provided for each chapter. Kerygma groups have been successfully led with the lecture and

discussion format or with an emphasis on participatory activities. There is, however, overwhelming evidence that adult learning is increased and enhanced when group members participate directly in the learning process. It is strongly recommended that all leaders review the session plans and incorporate as many suggestions as appropriate into each session.

Planning the Group Sessions

The first group session will be most effective if you distribute copies of the *Resource Book* to members of the group ahead of time. Tell them to read the Introduction and Chapter One and to bring any questions that arise from the reading to the session.

As you prepare your Session Plan, keep in mind that only you know the unique situation of your group: the number of participants; the amount of time for each session; the interests, abilities, and needs of each participant; and circumstances of the ministry of your church. Thus, you are the only one who can prepare a session plan that is truly appropriate for your particular group.

In your plan you will want to give special attention to the following elements that appear at the beginning of each chapter of the *Resource Book*.

1. *Summary*. This is the focus of the chapter. All that you and the participants will do during the group session will be done to uncover the meaning of the summary statement.

2. *Basic Bible References*. These are the essential references that you and the participants must read. These Bible texts provide the basis for the group session. They will be used in one or another of the suggested activities.

3. *Word List*. These words or phrases are important terms included in the biblical texts of the study. They may be unfamiliar to many members of your group. Yet they are words for which you, as the leader, should have working definitions.

The Session Plans in the *Leader's Guide* include:

1. *Learning Objectives*. The three or four statements presenting learning objectives indicate what the leader will help the participants to accomplish as a result of their study. It is appropriate to share these objectives with the members of the group at the beginning of each session. The selection of activities is then guided by the objectives considered most important. The learning objectives can also be used as a basis for evaluating whether you and the participants have accomplished what was intended. A word of caution: accomplishing the learning objectives is not all there is to leading a study group. Some of the most important

things that happen among the participants cannot be evaluated by learning objectives: things such as forming a Christian community, growing in faith, developing the ability to speak comfortably about one's faith, nurturing the spiritual life, and other important matters regarding the Christian faith.

2. *Resources You May Need.* In addition to the Bible, *Resource Book,* and supplementary readings, a list of those resources that are needed for the various activities is provided.

3. *Leadership Strategy.* This is the heart of the session plan. The leadership strategy is organized in three sections:

   a. "Setting the Stage" is a time for inviting persons to become involved with the subject of the session. Ordinarily it will take ten to fifteen minutes for this segment of the session.

   b. "Exploring the Scripture" is what the study is all about. Most of the time of the session will be spent with activities that involve exploration of biblical texts which are integral to the theme. Usually two or three activities will be planned for this portion of the session.

   c. "Closing" is a time to bring closure to the session, to summarize what has been explored, and to suggest applications of what has been learned to one's own faith and life experiences.

4. *Looking Ahead.* In order to work effectively at the next session, some or all of the participants may need to do some special preparation. For example, a brief report requiring some research is occasionally called for in the session plans. Participants are invited to volunteer for these assignments. Of course, the basic assignment for each week is reading the *Resource Book* and the recommended Bible texts.

5. *Additional Readings.* This is not a separate section in the Session Plans, but occasionally selections from supplementary volumes will be recommended to provide additional background for the material in the *Resource Book.* You may also want to consult some of the books listed at the end of Chapter Six in the *Resource Book.*

Using Leadership Strategies

As you read the suggestions in each Leadership Strategy, you will notice that several activities are usually offered for each segment of the session. These activities are clearly separated by **or, and,** or **and/or** in the center of the page. Ordinarily no group would be expected to complete all the activities that are included for each session. And there will be times when you, as the leader, will decide to do something different from what is suggested. You should feel free to utilize your own creativity, but be sure that what you do relates directly to the theme and learning objectives of the session.

When choosing from among the options that are suggested, there are several things to keep in mind.

1. The *amount of time* available is a critical factor which will influence your decision. When faced with the choice of trying to do two activities quickly (perhaps superficially) or doing one activity thoroughly, it is usually best to do the one activity.

2. *Activities that involve participants* interacting with one another, preparing a presentation to share with others, or working cooperatively on a task, will always take more time than it takes for the leader to present the same information. However, when persons are significantly involved in the process of their own learning, they will be much more motivated and will accomplish more in the end.

3. Some activities are designed to probe *in depth*, and others are intended to provide an *overview*. In addition, there are activities for individuals or pairs or small groups or the whole group. The important thing is to develop a session plan that has balance, so that there are some in-depth and some overview activities. There also needs to be a balance among individual, small group, and whole group activities.

4. The *interests, abilities,* and *previous experience* of the members of the group will influence your choices regarding which of the suggested activities to implement. It is important for you to become acquainted with the members of the group in order to make such judgments. It may be self-defeating to plan an activity that you feel will be resisted by many in the group.

5. Your own *interests, skills,* and *concerns* must also be considered when deciding which activity to choose. You should be reasonably comfortable with the activity and confident that it can be used effectively to guide the group's study. However, as the course develops and you become comfortable with the group and the subject matter, you should be willing to try some of the activities that are new to you.

Planning for leading a study group is an art. There is no right session plan for every topic or every situation or every leader. Neither is there just one right way to go about planning. You need to be willing to practice the art of planning until you find a process that works effectively for you.

A Final Word

You are about to embark on a wonderful journey with a number of companions. This time together has the potential for building relationships among those who participate, for increasing their knowledge and appreciation of the Lord's Prayer, and for providing a time of spiritual nurture and renewal. May this be a time of fruitful study and reflection for you and those who join you on the journey.

Introducing John Purdy

Mr. Purdy is a graduate of the College of Wooster (B.A.) and Princeton Theological Seminary (M.Div.). He also spent a year of study in Basel, Switzerland. Following seminary, Mr. Purdy was a pastor in Wisconsin for twelve years. For the next twenty-six years he was Curriculum Editor for the Presbyterian Church (U.S.A.). He is now retired but continues to write for publication.

He is the author of *Parables at Work* (Westminster Press, 1985) and *Returning God's Call: The Challenge of Christian Living* (Westminster Press, 1989) and the editor of the volume *Always Being Reformed: The Future of Church Education* (Geneva Press, 1985).

Additional Leadership Resources

In addition to the preceding suggestions, Kerygma has available several resources which will assist you in developing your leadership skills. The two books listed below are available from the Kerygma office.

Session Planning Form This form provides a key to help you organize your plans for each session. It is found on the next page. Feel free to make as many copies as you need. All courses include "Learning Objectives" except Discovering The Bible which substitutes the term "Session Purpose".

Guidelines for Adult Education These guidelines summarize ten general principles on which contemporary effective adult education is based. They will be found in an appendix at the back of this book.

Adult Education Idea Book A resource providing a comprehensive, design for establishing an effective program of adult education. It includes chapters on "Leadership and Leadership Development" and "Fifty Great Ideas to Help Promote Adult Bible Study in Your Church".

Basic Skills for Church Teachers by Donald L. Griggs. A resource for those wishing to improve teaching skills. Its insights apply to both children and adults and include sections on "The Art of Asking Questions" and "Enabling Creativity".

Kerygma Leader's Session Planning Form

Course Name _____ Leader _____

Session _____ Date _____ Time _____

Learning Objectives:

Real Time (i.e. 7:30 - 7:40)	Strategies/Activities	Resources Needed

Real Time (i.e. 7:30 - 7:40)	Strategies/Activities	Resources Needed

CHAPTER ONE

Keeping Our Distance

NOTES FROM THE AUTHOR

In my years of writing a monthly "Question and Answer" column for a denominational magazine, two inquiries have been very frequent: Why do some traditions say "debts" instead of "trespasses" in the Lord's Prayer? What principles ought to guide the use of the sanctuary and other parts of our church building?

The use of debts and debtors will be taken up in the fourth chapter of this study. The use of the church building is relevant to this first session. The question is asked in several different ways. One church member wanted to know about the propriety of allowing secular or controversial groups to meet in her church. Another wanted to know if it was alright to remove the communion table to accommodate a large wedding party. A third person wanted to know if square dancing in the church basement should be allowed.

Some church members have a feeling, which is difficult for them to articulate, that certain places and things ought to be regarded as sacred. They are not comfortable with the ease with which many contemporary Christians—including some pastors—set aside as old fashioned any notions of special days, words, space, artifacts. Many of them are equally uneasy with efforts to heighten the mood of worshipers with sentimental music, overly reverent voices, and special language. And yet they want attention paid to what is properly regarded as holy.

In this first study session on the Lord's Prayer, the ruling concept is that of holiness. Holiness in the biblical sense has as its root meaning, "separateness." A holy people is a people set apart. Holy things are set apart from the ordinary. A holy God is one from whom we keep a proper distance.

More than you might suppose, Protestant Christians are prepared to discuss the proper meaning of holiness. They may have been taught by their parents and pastors to be skeptical about holy water, holy beads, holy days, holy offices, and holy men and women. Some of them, as I once did, may have had experiences with Holiness sects, which have left them even more skeptical. But despite previous experiences and training, many church members know instinctively that you must allow for holiness.

This session of your study may seem the least relevant of the six. However, it will repay diligent effort. In both the Old and New Testament passages, holiness is treated as a life and death matter. One does not have to be tight-lipped and grim in leading a discussion of holiness. It is a very real concern for many people, and they will appreciate having this concern taken seriously.

SESSION PLANS

Learning Objectives

This session is intended to enable participants to:

1. Become acquainted with other members of the group.

2. Become familiar with the scheme for the study as outlined in the *Resource Book*.

3. Identify the biblical understanding of holiness which underlies the Basic Bible References for this chapter.

4. Describe in their own words the meaning of the petition, "Hallowed be your name."

Resources You May Need

Name tags and markers
Newsprint or a chalkboard and chalk
Sets of crayons
Copies of questions for the study of Mark 2:23-28
Copies of Mark 3:1-6 for the role play

Leadership Strategy

SETTING THE STAGE

1. If members of the group are new to one another, distribute name tags or some other means of identification as they enter the room.

   Begin the session with an opening prayer, praising God and asking the Spirit to be present in the session.

   Then go around the group and invite the members to identify themselves. Ask them to say a word about why they are taking the course and/or to recall the time when they first became acquainted with the Lord's Prayer.

2. If *Resource Books* have not been distributed prior to this first session, do that now. Allow time for participants to leaf through them to examine the chapter headings and format. Invite their attention to the Table of Contents. Note that a question about a key issue is provided for each chapter. Tell them it is expected that before each session they will have read not only the appropriate chapter in the *Resource Book,* but also the two primary biblical passages—one from the Old Testament and one from the New Testament. Indicate that the Scripture references in the *Resource Book* are all taken from the *New Revised Standard Version* of the Bible. Point out the value of comparing several translations of the Bible and encourage those who are devoted to versions other than the NRSV to share alternate readings with the group when appropriate.

   Then ask everyone to turn to the section in the Introduction entitled "The Plan of This Study." Summarize this material and the objectives Mr. Purdy describes for the course on page 4. Review the material on preparing for the first session and add comments from your own experience in preparing for this course or others like it.

   or

   If members of the group received their books at an earlier time, ask them to list any questions which arose from their reading in preparation for this session. Record these on newsprint. Also ask the group members for questions they have about the Lord's Prayer which they would like to discuss during the course. List these with the other questions. Then review the list, respond to any questions which are introductory in nature and note others which you will include in this session.

EXPLORING THE SCRIPTURE

1. As a way of introducing the discussion of the first petition of the Lord's Prayer, invite volunteers to share memories of how Sunday was observed when they were children. What made this day special and different from other days?

and

Write the word "holy" at the top of a sheet of newsprint and post it at the front of the room. Ask group members to suggest words or phrases which are similar or which help to define holy. Record these on the newsprint. Then invite persons to compare the terms and to describe the basic concept or idea which underlies our understanding of holiness.

and/or

In Notes from the Author, Mr. Purdy suggests that in the Old Testament the root meaning of holiness is "separateness." Present a two or three minute word study on holy or holiness, summarizing material from a Bible dictionary or a theological wordbook.

2. Invite participants to turn to Exodus 19:1-20:21. Ask them to read the passage and to note any sections which deal with distance and space. List the group's discoveries on newsprint and add any additional instances you have noted.

For example:

Exodus 19:1-6 refers to the journey from Egypt to the mountain in Sinai.

Exodus 19:10-15 describes how the people are not to go too close to the mountain.

Exodus 19:16-25 tells how the people came near the mountain, but were warned not to come up the mountain to attempt to see God.

Then direct the group's attention to the commandment about keeping the sabbath in Exodus 20:8-11. Ask the group members how the references to space and distance they noted above are related to this commandment. Or, summarize Mr. Purdy's comments about this relationship on pages 8-9 of the *Resource Book*.

and/or

Divide the group into subgroups of four to six persons. Each subgroup is to review Exodus 19:1-20:21 and to draw a picture on newsprint, summarizing the story. Provide newsprint and markers or crayons for each subgroup.

After about twenty minutes, have each subgroup present its picture to the whole group, noting any special features of the story it has included in its drawing.

Invite everyone to turn to Exodus 20:8-11 and ask the group how the events it has portrayed are related to the commandment about keeping the sabbath. How is Israel's holiness as a nation dependent upon remembering to observe every seventh day as a "workless" day?

3. Present a brief minilecture on the laws for sabbath observance which the Pharisees in Jesus' day had developed. Then retell the stories in Mark 2:23-28 and 3:1-6, indicating why the Pharisees were angry at Jesus.

or

Divide the group into pairs. Give each pair a copy of the following questions and ask it to respond to these after reading Mark 2:23-28.

a. What did Jesus and his disciples do that aroused the anger of the Pharisees?

b. Why was this action so offensive to the Pharisees? What idea or concept is at the heart of their rage at Jesus' apparent disregard for sabbath regulations? (See "A Life and Death Matter" on page 11 of the *Resource Book*.)

c. How did Jesus answer his critics?

d. How do you interpret Jesus' comment that "the sabbath was made for humankind, and not humankind for the sabbath"?

and

Do a simple role play of Mark 3:1-6. Let one participant take the part of the person with the withered hand, another the part of Jesus, three of the group the parts of the Pharisees, and the rest be simply onlookers in the synagogue. Begin the role play by having one of the Pharisees testify to having been present near the grain field earlier in the day and having seen the disciples eating the grain. Let another Pharisee then charge Jesus with being a sabbath-breaker. Let Jesus answer that charge. Then let him be approached by the person with the withered hand and play out the rest of the scene, including a brief meeting of the three Pharisees, who discuss why they need to get rid of Jesus.

After the role play, discuss the feelings the different characters in the story would have experienced. Why would the Pharisees not approve of a charitable act such as healing on the sabbath?

4. Write the phrase "Hallowed be your name" on a sheet of newsprint. According to Mr. Purdy, this petition is a plea for God to maintain a proper distance between us. Remind the group that Mr. Purdy says this distance is "a life and death matter." Invite members of the group to comment on how the seriousness of this petition is illustrated in the narratives from Exodus and Mark. (See pages 11-12 in the *Resource Book*.)

Ask for suggestions of other words in which this first petition of the Lord's Prayer might be expressed. (For example, "Protect your name.") Write these on the newsprint and invite the group to discuss the merits of each alternative.

and/or

On pages 2-3 in the Introduction to the *Resource Book*, Mr. Purdy notes the "two-tiered" structure of the Lord's Prayer: we are invited to approach God as children coming to a loving parent, but the God whom we approach is also the Holy One of Israel. Keeping both these thoughts in mind is part of maintaining the proper distance in prayer.

Divide the group into two sections. One section is to think about what happens to prayer when we approach God in a cavalier manner. The other group is to reflect on the problems which occur when God remains too abstract or distant.

Invite those in each section to share their reflections. List them on newsprint. Discuss how the first line of the Lord's Prayer, "Our Father in heaven," and the petition "Hallowed be your name," help us to maintain a balance in our prayers.

CLOSING

1. Discuss the possibility of saving the final five minutes of each session for a time of prayer. If that seems agreeable, suggest that the group members follow these instructions for a closing prayer:

They will close their eyes and assume an attitude of prayer, while you read aloud the following:

"We are standing together on a vast plain. Ahead of us a mountain thrusts high into the air. The top of the mountain is surrounded by mist. We have been told that this is the mountain where God dwells, where heaven and earth actually meet. We are not permitted to see God, but we are permitted to call to God, assured that God will answer. From the mountain we hear the sound of the angelic choir, singing:

"Holy, Holy, Holy! Lord God Almighty!
Early in the morning our song shall rise to Thee;

Holy, Holy, Holy! merciful and mighty!
God in three Persons, blessed Trinity."

And we respond together in the words Jesus taught us, "Our Father in heaven, hallowed be your name…"

or

As your closing prayer, read aloud the words of the familiar hymn "Holy, Holy, Holy!" (Nothing has so shaped Protestant spirituality as the hymnbook. You may decide that you will use familiar hymns for your closing prayers.)

Looking Ahead

1. In activity #1 under Exploring the Scripture in the next session, it is suggested that a volunteer compose two entries that Samuel might have written in a personal journal during the time of the confrontation with the leaders of Israel described in 1 Samuel 8. See the activity for details.

CHAPTER TWO

Crossing to the Future

NOTES FROM THE AUTHOR

The members of the committee that produced *An Inclusive Language Lectionary* for the National Council of Churches had a difficult time with the term "Kingdom of God" (or its equivalent, "Kingdom of Heaven"). They most often rendered it as "realm of God." Occasionally they chose "Sovereignty of God" as an alternative. In their version of the Lord's Prayer in Luke, they have given us "May your dominion come." (Luke 11:2b) The Lectionary committee wanted to break with the gender-specific imagery of a state of affairs presided over by a male.

In his preaching and teaching about the kingdom of God, Jesus wanted to break with the notion of the restoration of the Israelite monarchy. In the parables of the kingdom collected in Matthew 13, there is nothing to suggest that the kingdom will arrive through statecraft, military conquest, revolution, or reform. Rather, Jesus describes the better future arriving like yeast working in flour, like a seed growing in the ground, like a farmer sowing a crop, like a treasure discovered in a field, and like a merchant hunting for pearls.

If we assume Jesus' familiarity with the Hebrew Scriptures, then we may well suppose that he had learned an important lesson from the history of Israel. According to 1 Samuel 8, the people of Israel were not long established in the Promised Land before they turned it into a kingdom like those of their neighbors. The concept of a holy people, defended and ruled by Yahweh, was replaced with that of a nation state ruled by a divinely appointed monarch. The elders of Israel said: "We are determined to have a king over us, so that we also may be like other nations." (1 Samuel 8:19-20a) And a king was what they got.

Throughout history other peoples have been equally determined to shape a promising future in terms of models already at hand. Hopes for justice and security and prosperity get frozen into ideologies—as the failures of Communism in Eastern Europe so graphically remind us. Even the hope for the realm of God becomes frozen into a social system, a program for reform, a political philosophy. The pattern established in 1 Samuel 8 is repeated over and over again. The plea, "Your kingdom come," is not very different from a political slogan or a party platform.

The challenge of the second petition of the Lord's Prayer is to our understanding of history. Any attempt to freeze the present or to return to the past would seem to be acts of unfaithfulness to God. Jesus has pointed us to a genuinely new, truly better future. At least that is what the juxtaposition of 1 Samuel 8 and Matthew 13 seem to teach us.

SESSION PLANS

Learning Objectives

This session is intended to enable participants to:

1. Describe the origin of kingship in Israel, according to 1 Samuel 8.

2. Briefly interpret at least one parable from Matthew 13 that seems consistent with the second petition of the Lord's Prayer.

3. Suggest several ways in which praying, "Your kingdom come" will involve doing God's work in the world.

Resources You May Need

Newsprint and markers, or a chalkboard and chalk

An Inclusive Language Lectionary, Year A, B, or C or photocopies of the paragraph from the Lectionary printed on the following page

Scripts for a dramatic reading of 1 Samuel 8

Leadership Strategy

SETTING THE STAGE

1. Welcome any participants who were not present for the first session. Bring them up to speed by a quick summary of the progress of that session. (This will be useful for all members of the group.) Then lead the group in an opening prayer.

2. Make it a practice at the beginning of each session to ask participants for any questions that surfaced in their preparatory reading. Record these on newsprint or a chalkboard and decide when to take them up in the session. This has several advantages: (1) It shows that you expect members of the group to have studied the Bible and the *Resource Book* beforehand. (2) It shows that you take their questions seriously. (3) It helps you as the leader to prepare for the next session. You can assess how well your teaching strategy met the needs and expectations of the learners.

3. Mention *An Inclusive Language Lectionary,* published by the National Council of Churches. It was designed to provide for reading in public worship a version of the Bible that was less gender-specific in references to God and humans. It is not necessary that you yourself be familiar with the *Lectionary* or that you have copies on hand, although that would be useful. But at least, describe the various choices faced by the authors in their translation of the Greek word that is represented as "kingdom" in the Lord's Prayer. Either by reading aloud or by handing out photocopies, share the following explanation that is found in the appendix of the *Lectionary:*

   The Greek word used frequently in the New Testament, and usually translated by the gender-specific word "kingdom," has generally been rendered in this lectionary as "realm," although it has been translated by other terms as well. The Greek word refers either to the activity of God (i.e., God's "kingship" or "dominion" or "reign" or "rule,") or to the state of affairs brought about by God (i.e., God's "kingdom" or "dominion" or "realm"). The Hebrew root usually translated "kingdom" in the RSV is occasionally rendered "kingdom" in this lectionary, but is also rendered by other terms such as "sovereignty" or "rule".

   Write on newsprint or a chalkboard various possible renderings of the second petition of the Lord's Prayer, e.g., "your kingdom come," "may your dominion come," "your realm come," "may your rule be established." Discuss the suggestion offered on pages 22-23 of the *Resource Book* that we might vary the language we use in the second petition of the Lord's Prayer, sometimes using the language of kingdom, sometimes using the language of sovereignty, realm, rule, or dominion. What are some of the consequences, both for personal devotions and for public worship, of deliberately departing from a fixed format? You don't need to resolve this issue. Be content to identify the value of the different options.

EXPLORING THE SCRIPTURE

1. Stage a dramatic reading of 1 Samuel 8. Ask one person to read the remarks of the narrator, one to read the part of Samuel, and another to read the part of Yahweh. Ask several others to read the words of the elders and the people.

   While these members of the group are preparing the reading, list these questions on newsprint or a chalkboard:

   a. What prompted the elders to ask for a king?

   b. What was God's response to their request?

   c. What was Samuel's objection to the request?

   Divide the remaining participants into three listening teams and assign each team one question. At the conclusion of the reading the teams are to report what they heard in response to their questions.

   or

   Introduce the person who volunteered at the last session to compose two entries Samuel might have made in his personal journal during the confrontation with the elders of Israel. A review of Chapters 4-8 in 1 Samuel and information from a Bible dictionary on the rise of kingship in Israel will be helpful in carrying out this assignment. One entry should be based on the material in 1 Samuel 8:4-9; the other should reflect the dialogue in the remainder of the chapter.

   and

   In Notes from the Author, Mr. Purdy says the result of Israel's desire for a king was that "The concept of a holy people, defended and ruled by Yahweh, was replaced with that of a nation state ruled by a divinely appointed monarch." Discuss how this comment illustrates the different views of kingship evident in 1 Samuel 8. Ask how Israel's desire to be like other nations influenced how people in Jesus' day heard his message about the coming of God's kingdom.

2. Now move to a consideration of Jesus' parables about the kingdom. Ask the group from what sources—biblical, historical, personal—Jesus might have derived his understanding of the "kingdom." What might have been some common concepts of kingdom in the minds of his hearers? Of Matthew?

Invite participants to name the various similes for the kingdom in Matthew 13, e.g., seed sown, a net cast, yeast mixed into flour. List these on newsprint or a chalkboard. Then ask a series of questions designed to compare and contrast these figures of speech.

   a. Do you detect any common threads running through all the comparisons? If so, what are they?

   b. Can you arrange the phrases in clusters, grouping those that seem to fit most closely together? What comparisons are included in each cluster?

   c. Do any of the similes seem contradictory? If so, which ones and in what ways?

or

List all of the comparisons in Matthew 13 on newsprint or a chalkboard. Ask participants to select their favorite ones and indicate their choices by a show of hands. Record the results of the poll by placing the number of votes beside each phrase. Ask persons to share the reasons for their selection.

and

Invite members of the group to create their own parables of the kingdom. Remind them that Jesus' parables are not based on past political models but have a future orientation. Suggest figures of speech such as a scientific discovery or a spaceship journey. What other figures can the group create?

3. By using parables, Jesus provided indirect descriptions rather than a blueprint of the kingdom. However, as Mr. Purdy points out on page 21 of the *Resource Book*, "God's intentions for us are quite plain." One of the places those intentions are described is Micah 6:8, where doing justice, loving kindness, and walking humbly with God, are mentioned.

Divide the group into three smaller groups. Each group is to take one of the admonitions from Micah and discuss what it might mean for Christians today. The groups may want to review the material on pages 21-22 of the *Resource Book* for suggestions. After several minutes, have each group summarize its discussion for the others.

or

Lead a discussion of the reasons why Jesus used parables to describe the kingdom rather than more literal language. You will find helpful material on pages 19-22 of the *Resource Book* and in Notes from the Author. How does this practice enable us to be critical of efforts to shape the future in terms of models already at hand? In what way does it open us to work for the new future God is bringing?

CLOSING

1. Ask participants to close their eyes and be prepared to say the Lord's Prayer in response to what you are about to suggest. Then describe in some detail an immigrant group that is crossing a broad and swift river into the land of its hopes and dreams. Describe the land which the group has just left—the things that begin to look pretty good in retrospect. Tell about some of the good things it has heard about the land on the far side of the river. Describe the difficulties with the crossing: the slippery rocks that challenge footing, the fear of being swept down the river, the panic of those who cannot swim. Conclude your description with the three stanzas of the hymn, "Guide Me, O Thou Great Jehovah"—using the plural instead of the singular, e.g., "Guide Us, O Thou Great Jehovah, Pilgrims in This Barren Land." Then invite participants to join in praying the Lord's Prayer (after agreeing in advance what language you will use for the second petition).

or

As your closing prayer, use the words to the hymn, "Guide Me, O Thou Great Jehovah," which in the third stanza refers to crossing the Jordan into a better country. And invite the group to join in saying the Lord's Prayer—after you have agreed on what phrasing you will use for the second petition.

Looking Ahead

1. Suggest that for reading extensive passages of the Bible it is helpful to draw a chart of the passage, writing headings for each paragraph and attempting a title for the entire section. For example:

Jesus and the Law

Matthew 5

1-12	How to be Happy
13-16	Universal Mission
17-20	Fulfilling the Law
21-26	Reconciliation
27-30	Looking with Lust
31-32	No Divorce!
33-37	No Oaths!
38-42	No Retribution
43-48	Be Like God

2. In activity #1 under Exploring the Scripture in the next session, it is suggested that a member of the group present a minilecture on the background, structure, and content of the Holiness Code. See the activity for details.

CHAPTER THREE

Willing Obedience

NOTES FROM THE AUTHOR

Look at the story about the wind and the windmill on page 33 in the *Resource Book*. It illustrates the intellectual challenge of any discussion of "Your will be done, on earth as it is in heaven." If you were teaching a class in philosophy, you might set forth the arguments of determinism vs. free will. In church circles the choices tend to be presented in different terms. A piety featuring submission to everything that happens as the will of God is set off against a piety that lays stress on making every activity a doing of God's will. The first kind of piety is crudely dismissed by its critics as pure fatalism; the second kind is dismissed by its critics as unfounded pride in human ability.

The French writer, Simone Weil, has framed the old categories in a different way. She has written of gravity and grace. What we perceive of the created world, including human behavior, obeys certain laws or rules. We humans are no more exempt from "gravity" than are stars and stones. But there is always the possibility of grace, of what Weil calls "supernatural intervention," by which humans are able—as it were—to think and act in ways that defy gravity.

What tends to get lost in such considerations is this: What is it that God wills? If indeed a sovereign God rules and overrules in all that happens, to what end or purpose does God do all these things? And if we humans are free to carry out God's intentions on earth, what are those intentions? If God has made known the divine purpose, that revelation ought to make a good deal of difference in how we discuss determinism and free will, sovereignty and individual responsibility, gravity and grace.

Therefore, in the *Resource Book* the suggestion is made that in the third petition of the Lord's Prayer we ask for several things at once. We ask that God's purposes be accomplished. We ask that these purposes be accomplished through us. And we also ask that they be accomplished in spite of us.

It will be helpful to you, in leading this session, to emphasize that terms like "the will of God" and "the Law of God" are best understood in terms of God's purposes, intentions, and revealed goals for the creation. Often confusion and conflict arise when persons insist on representing God's will in terms of specific regulations. For example, there are some who will argue: "God does not will that homosexuals are to be ministers." "God does not want people to drink alcoholic beverages." "God does not want people to work on the sabbath."

It is true enough that in Scripture sometimes God's will and purpose are expressed in terms of rules. The Fourth Commandment would seem to be such. But as suggested in Session One, the idea of a sabbath rest is grounded in God's nature and purpose. Always, always, we need to look behind the rule or regulation for God's intentions. Otherwise we lapse into legalism.

In discussing passages of Scripture such as Leviticus 19, one way to make sense of the material and to profit from it is to look for the intention of God that may be revealed in a particular rule. As a guide to this process, it is helpful to keep in mind three categories of moral or ethical standards: (1) rules and regulations, (2) principles and precepts, and (3) divine purposes and intentions. Rules and regulations provide very specific direction. For example, there is the rule against working on the sabbath. A principal or precept expresses the rationale which underlies a rule or regulation. This rule against work on the sabbath is based on the precept that the sabbath is a day of rest. And the sabbath rest is, in turn, grounded in God's intention or purpose to create and sustain human life.

This may get you deeper into moral philosophy than you want to go! But it is better to step into deep water, already fitted out with even a crude life preserver, than to fall into it with no warning and no support.

SESSION PLANS

Learning Objectives

This session is intended to enable participants to:

1. Cite examples of rules, precepts and purposes in Leviticus 19 and Matthew 5.

2. Recall two or three instances where Jesus offers a new perspective on an old precept in Matthew 5.

3. Describe some of the difficulties encountered in offering willing obedience to God.

Resources You May Need

Newsprint and markers or a chalkboard and chalk
A hymnbook

Leadership Strategy

SETTING THE STAGE

1. Open the session with a prayer. Then take up any unfinished business left at the end of the last meeting. If some questions raised in that session were left unanswered, answer them now. Use this opportunity to summarize what was discussed and decided up to this point.

and/or

Many experienced adult leaders share with their groups at the beginning of each session the learning objectives for that session. Some will have them written on newsprint or the chalkboard and will review them briefly with the group. This is the leader's way of saying: "This is *my* agenda. This is what I am prepared to get done." This gives the group confidence that it is in firm hands. Also, when the leader invites the participants to ask questions about the advance assignment, the group is not left to wonder if the session will be nothing but a free discussion.

and

Remind the group of the story of the Friends' Meeting on page 33 of the *Resource Book*. Ask for a volunteer to tell the story. (If no one remembers the story, read it aloud from the *Resource Book*.) Invite participants to suggest other figures of speech that show the relationship of divine initiative and human response. You may want to "prime the pump" by asking participants to complete the following statements:

God is the fire. The church is the wood. We had better ...

God is the rain. The church is the field. We had better ...

God is the employer. The church is the employee. We had better ...

God is the potter. The church is the clay. We had better ...

EXPLORING THE SCRIPTURE

Lucia

1. Present a minilecture on the background, purpose, structure, and content of the Holiness Code, or introduce the person who volunteered for this task at the last session. You will find helpful material in a Bible dictionary and *Understanding the Old Testament* by Bernard Anderson. Be sure to point out how specific rules and precepts are related to the purpose of the Code stated in Leviticus 19:2.

or

Suggest to the group that one way of understanding God's will is to use the three categories of moral or ethical standards mentioned in Notes from the Author: rules/regulations, precepts/principles, and purposes/intentions. Write these categories as headings on a chalkboard or at the top of three separate sheets of newsprint. Indicate that the discussion in the previous session about the kingdom of God had to do with God's purposes or intentions. Point out that God's will is also revealed in Scripture in the other two categories

Then invite participants to open their Bibles to Leviticus 19 and to find examples of both rules and principles. As participants identify these, list them on the separate sheets of newsprint or in columns on a chalkboard. For example, Leviticus 19:3 is obviously a principle/precept, while verses 5-8 constitute regulations about sacrifices. Go through the entire chapter and see if you can distinguish regulations from precepts. (Admittedly, there will be some disagreement about how to categorize certain verses.)

and

Ask the group to look for some expression in this chapter of the purpose or intention of God. Are there any statements where such a purpose or intention is indicated? If no responses are forthcoming, point out the recurrence of the phrase, "I am the LORD." (Verses 3, 4, 10, 12, etc.) Suggest that this phrase is linked to the declaration in verse 2, "You shall be holy, for I the LORD your God am holy." This opening statement announces the purpose of the Holiness Code.

2. Ask the participants to open their Bibles to Matthew 5. Point out to the group examples from each of the categories suggested for analyzing the contents of Leviticus 19—rules/regulations, precepts/principles, purposes/intentions. (For example, in the Beatitudes Jesus pronounces several principles of life in God's realm. In the balance of the chapter he cites and reinterprets a number of regulations from the Old Testament.) Provide illustrations of how Leviticus and Matthew deal with the same issues. Include some examples of how Jesus

provided a new "slant" on an old precept. Indicate how Matthew 5:48 is the climax of the chapter.

or

Ask participants to carry out the same activity with Matthew 5 that was suggested above for Leviticus 19—go through and identify rules/regulations, precepts/principles, and divine purposes/intentions. Place these three categories on separate sheets of newsprint or a chalkboard and lead the group in listing the appropriate sections of Matthew 5 under each category. Or, if you have enough time, assign three smaller groups to work with the three categories and to report their work to the whole group.

and

If the group completed the above exercise with Leviticus 19, compare the lists from that chapter with the ones from Mathew 5. Ask for examples of where Leviticus and Matthew deal with the same human concerns. Invite participants to point out where Jesus develops a new interpretation of a precept. For example, compare the passages below:

> You shall not hate in your heart anyone of your kin; you shall reprove your neighbor, or you will incur guilt upon yourself. You shall not take vengeance or bear a grudge against any of your people, but you shall love your neighbor as yourself: I am the LORD. (Leviticus 19:17-18)

> You have heard that it was said, "You shall love your neighbor and hate your enemy." But I say to you, Love your enemies and pray for those who persecute you, so that you may be children of your Father in heaven; for he makes his sun rise on the evil and on the good, and sends rain on the righteous and on the unrighteous. For if you love those who love you, what reward do you have? Do not even the tax collectors do the same? And if you greet only your brothers and sisters, what more are you doing than others? Do not even the Gentiles do the same? Be perfect, therefore, as your heavenly Father is perfect. (Matthew 5:43-48)

3. Write on newsprint or a chalkboard the primary purpose statements from Leviticus 19 and Matthew 5:

> You shall be holy,
>> for I the LORD your God am holy. (Leviticus 19:2)

Be perfect, therefore,

as your heavenly Father is perfect. (Matthew 5:48)

Ask: Are these both "counsels of perfection" which none of us have any hope of following? If they are not, how are we to understand them? At this point, elicit from the group views about the difficulty, even the possibility, of doing God's will on earth. You may also want to ask for a show of hands in response to two questions:

How many believe it is possible for humans to obey God in all areas of their lives?

How many believe that no matter what humans do, they are certain to fall short of what God intends?

Discuss the meaning of the results of the poll.

and

Ask participants what relationships they see among Leviticus 19:2, Matthew 5:48, and the third petition of the Lord's Prayer, "Your will be done, on earth as it is in heaven." Then invite them to rewrite the third petition in terms of either the statement from Leviticus or the one from Matthew. For example:

May we here on earth lead holy lives, just as you in heaven are holy.

May your divine perfection be duplicated on earth.

Discuss the appropriateness of such phrasing.

or

On pages 30-32 of the *Resource Book* and in the Notes from the Author for this chapter, Mr. Purdy says that when we pray the third petition of the Lord's Prayer we are asking for at least three things:

- That God's purposes be accomplished

- That these purposes be accomplished through us

- That these purposes be accomplished in spite of us

Summarize the material in the *Resource Book* about these three requests. Or, if you have more time, divide the group into three smaller groups and assign one of the requests to each small group. They are to review the appropriate paragraphs on pages 30-32 of the *Resource Book* and compose a brief summary of their understanding of their requests.

Reconvene the whole group to hear the summaries. Allow for questions and comments from participants as each group reports.

CLOSING

1. Ask participants to close their eyes and assume an attitude of prayer. Then, drawing on the description of arroyos on pages 32-33 in the *Resource Book* and your own experiences of arid places, paint a word picture of a farm family waiting for the seasonal rains to fill the irrigation ditches and water the crops. Lead into the reading of the stanzas of a hymn such as "Spirit of God, Descend upon My Heart," "Have Thine Own Way, Lord," or some other hymn about the descent of the Spirit. Then lead the group in saying together the Lord's Prayer.

or

Use as your closing prayer the words to a hymn such as "Have Thine Own Way, Lord," "Whate'er My God Ordains is Right," or "Take My Life, and Let It Be Consecrated, Lord, to Thee."

Looking Ahead

1. Remind participants of the admonition of the theologian Karl Barth that Christians ought to read the newspaper along with the Bible in order to know what God is doing and wants done at the present time. Ask them to look for articles about hunger in their daily newspaper and to bring these to the next session. They will be used in activity #2 in Setting the Stage.

CHAPTER FOUR

Feeding Ourselves

NOTES FROM THE AUTHOR

The focus in this session is on remembering and forgetting. We all have selective memories. That fact is obvious in family disputes and court proceedings, where people give different accounts of the same events in their common past. Each of us constructs a unique history by a careful selection of remembrances.

In his Pulitzer Prize winner, *The Denial of Death*, anthropologist Ernest Becker dealt with a similar theme. He showed how we repress the knowledge that we are mortal: "The idea of death, the fear of it, haunts the human animal like nothing else; it is a mainspring of human activity—activity designed largely to avoid the fatality of death, to overcome it by denying in some way that it is the final destiny of man."

The Deuteronomist had observed some selective denying in Israel. The terrible days of privation in the wilderness had been forgotten. So also had Yahweh's outright gift of the land. Pride had replaced thankfulness. People had begun to look to other gods for favors, like spouses who forget their first love and look to other lovers. Deuteronomy 8 attempts to force a remembrance by Israel of its dependence on Yahweh. The call to remember is coupled with a paradoxical warning: those who forget their dependence will surely perish.

One of the events that the Deuteronomist remembers is the feeding of Israel with manna in the wilderness. Jesus' feeding of the four thousand is reminiscent of that earlier feeding. And the narrative in Mark 8 also presents us with a paradox. The Gospel miracles seem to be events in which universal laws are suspended. But in fact, the miracles are revelatory of universal truth. Jesus' resurrection is assurance that God grants eternal life. The healing of the sick is assurance that illness is not a punishment. And the feeding of the four thousand is testimony that it is God who feeds us. We do not feed ourselves. Like the sermon in Deuteronomy 8, this feeding is a reminder of what most of us would desperately like to forget: We are not immortal. We cannot secure our own lives. We cannot even feed ourselves.

Because it deals with themes of dependence, mortality, and forgetfulness, this session on the fourth petition will not be easy on the leader or the participants. It can be saved from hand-wringing by the remembrance of the three petitions already considered. The One to whom we look for food is the Holy One of Israel, whose purpose is justice and mercy, whose sovereign will prevails over all enemies, even death.

SESSION PLANS

Learning Objectives

This session is intended to enable participants to:

1. Indicate how Deuteronomy 8 and Mark 8:1-10 remind us that we cannot feed ourselves.

2. Describe their understanding of the fourth petition of the Lord's Prayer.

Resources You May Need

Newsprint and markers or a chalkboard and chalk
Directions for analyzing Deuteronomy 8 and Mark 8 in small groups
A hymnbook

Leadership Strategy

SETTING THE STAGE

1. Open the session with a prayer. Then follow the pattern you have already established for eliciting reactions to the reading assignment, identifying questions that need to be answered, and summarizing progress to this point in the study.

2. Write on newsprint or a chalkboard in separate columns the two tiers of petitions from the Lord's Prayer, e.g., "Hallowed be your name" at the top of one list, and "Give us this day our daily bread" at the top of the other. Remind participants what was said in the Introduction of the *Resource Book* about the difference between the first and second sections in the Lord's Prayer. The first section deals

with what God expects of us. The second section deals with what we may expect from God.

Suggest that we ought to pray the initial three petitions with our hand raised in a salute, but the next three with our hand held out to receive gifts. Perhaps lead the group in praying the Lord's Prayer in that manner. Point out the somewhat paradoxical nature of these two gestures—that in the same brief prayer we both promise loyalty and ask for help.

and/or

If participants were asked to collect articles about hunger at the close of the last session, have them share these now. They might also indicate how they or others in the community are involved in addressing this issue.

EXPLORING THE SCRIPTURE

1. The following activity can be done by the whole group or in two or three smaller groups. If you use small groups, provide a copy of the directions and newsprint and markers for each group. These groups should report the results of their work to the whole group after about fifteen minutes.

Ask the participants to open their Bibles to Deuteronomy 8. Write on newsprint the heading "God Sustains Human Life." Suggest this as the title for a sermon based on Deuteronomy 8. Invite everyone to read through the chapter and note ways God is reported to have sustained the people of Israel. Record these on newsprint or a chalkboard.

Suggest that a sermon usually contains at least three major points. Have the group select the items from the newsprint it wants to include in its sermon and discuss how these points might be interpreted to a present-day congregation.

Then ask participants to look for one summarizing verse which could furnish the text for the sermon. If no suggestions are forthcoming, offer as possibilities "One does not live by bread alone, but by every word that comes from the mouth of the LORD" (Deuteronomy 8:3b) or, "If you do forget the LORD your God and follow other gods to serve and worship them, I solemnly warn you today that you shall surely perish." (v. 19) Invite persons to indicate why they prefer one or the other text as the focus for the sermon.

or

Ask participants to go through Deuteronomy 8 and underline every reference to remembering and forgetting. Then invite them to assist you in listing on newsprint or a chalkboard what Israel is admonished to remember and not to forget. Then ask which of these items Christians need to be reminded of today. What words or phrases would you use to translate these admonitions into the contemporary situation?

2. Ask a volunteer to read aloud the story of the feeding of the four thousand in Mark 8:1-10. Work on ideas for a sermon from this chapter also, either in the whole group or in the smaller groups used above. Use the following questions for this task:

   a. If you were asked to preach a sermon on this story, what would you emphasize? (List the responses on newsprint.)

   b. What parts of the story would you leave out? Why?

   c. Would you tie this story to Deuteronomy 8? In what way?

   d. What is the central message you would want to convey in the sermon?

   e. How might the sermon link up with the articles about hunger reported in Setting the Stage?

and/or

Summarize on newsprint or a chalkboard the following ways in which Mark 8:1-10 might be understood in the life of the church:

   • It may be used to show the concern of God for the hungry.

   • It may be seen as a reminder of the feeding of the faithful in the bread and wine of the Lord's Supper.

   • It may be employed as an illustration of the power of prayer.

Invite participants to suggest additional interpretations. Then ask them to select the choices they prefer and indicate why.

3. Part of the meaning of the petition, "Give us this day our daily bread" is the basic fact of our existence: We cannot feed ourselves.

Ask members of the group to imagine persons in quite different circumstances praying the fourth petition of the Lord's Prayer. As you mention these different persons, ask participants to consider how each of these persons might understand this basic fact. Invite volunteers to share their responses with the group.

- An Ethiopian farmer whose children are dying in time of famine

- An overweight man sitting in a pew in a church in suburban Toronto

- A single parent on welfare in Oakland, anxious about unpaid bills

- A woman with a Ph.D. in agronomy, doing her daily devotions

- A ten-year old child saying her prayers before going to sleep

- A Senator or other public official attending church on Sunday

After the exercise, ask participants to suggest feelings or experiences which might be common to all of these persons.

and/or

On pages 40-42 of the *Resource Book* Mr. Purdy says that when we come to the fourth petition of the Lord's Prayer we would do well to imagine ourselves as soldiers on active duty who are requesting our daily rations.

Make a brief presentation to the group outlining other interpretations of this petition. (It is a call to return to a simple, unadorned style of life; it is a plea for relief from our anxiety about food, clothing, etc.) Compare these views with Mr. Purdy's understanding. In the process, explore how the various interpretations do or do not provide linkages to Deuteronomy 8 and Mark 8.

and

If you are using this study during Lent, remind participants that fasting during Lent is a practice some Christians continue to the present day. Ask the group: What might fasting help us to remember? What are the dangers of fasting? Why has the practice been abandoned by so many Christians?

If you have time, turn to the sample table grace included in item #3 of the Reflection section on page 44 of the *Resource Book*. Ask the question listed there about the appropriateness of this grace, in light of the discussion about daily bread.

1. If you have established the practice of suggesting a graphic image as preparation for praying the Lord's Prayer together, invite participants to assume the posture of prayer and paint this imaginary picture for them:

We have all been conscripted into a vast army. Our nation has been threatened by the forces of a terrible tyrant and we have prepared ourselves for war. We are all in uniform, whatever our rank. We have left behind spouses, children, jobs, parents, homes, communities. We all have dependents back home who need food and housing and medical care that we will not be on hand to provide.

Our own army is so huge that it requires enormous quantities of food and clothing for us and our fellow soldiers, as well as a mammoth supply system that is efficiently organized and run. We have a large medical corps, but it could be overwhelmed if the casualties are high. It is the eve of a decisive battle. Our chaplain leads us in praying the Lord's Prayer.

or

As a closing prayer, use the words of a hymn that is a setting for the Twenty-Third Psalm. Or, if you prefer, use a hymn such as "O God, Our Help in Ages Past," or "Break Thou the Bread of Life."

Looking Ahead

1. If you have established the practice of closing with a time of prayer in which you read an imaginary scenario, recruit a member of the group to prepare the description for the next session. Suggest that this person consider using a prison scene as provided in the *Resource Book*.

2. Invite each person to make a private list of the persons and institutions to whom money is owed and a list of those persons and institutions owing money to him or her. These lists are referred to in activity #2 in Setting the Stage.

3. In activity #1 under Exploring the Scripture it is suggested that a member of the group give a brief presentation on the Year of Jubilee. See the activity for details.

4. In activity #3 in the same section it is suggested that three persons give brief presentations about the advantages of using "trespasses," "debts," or "sins" in the Lord's Prayer. Again, see the description of the activity for additional information.

And forgive us our debts,
as we also have forgiven our debtors

(HAPTER FIVE

Writing It Off

NOTES FROM THE AUTHOR

In *The Cost of Discipleship*, Dietrich Bonhoeffer warns us against "cheap grace." Cheap grace is "forgiveness of sins proclaimed as a general truth ... the preaching of forgiveness without requiring repentance." Bonhoeffer pleads instead for costly grace. "Above all, it is costly because it cost God the life of his Son ... and what has cost God much cannot be cheap for us."

One advantage in using the term "debts" in the fifth petition of the Lord's Prayer is that it suggests a costly transaction. There is a price to be paid for forgiveness. It is not just an inward feeling of good will and tolerance and acceptance. It is a personal transaction that exacts from us a price.

We read the account of the Jubilee Year in Leviticus 25, and it sounds like a great giveaway. Land is returned to former owners; indentured servants are set free; debts are forgiven. But someone pays a considerable price—the person who returns the land, releases the servant, remits the debt. Freedom is not free; forgiveness is costly. That is the important biblical insight we can gain from the Jubilee Year.

And the idea that there is some sort of cost attached to forgiveness is reinforced by Jesus' parable of the unforgiving servant in Matthew 18:21-35. The difference between the debt this servant was forgiven and the debt he would not himself forgive is enormous. It is so enormous as to be ridiculous. He was handed a gift of millions, and to receive it he had only to make a slight gesture—no more effortful than the closing of the fist. But he could not make that slight gesture, and so he lost everything.

The fifth petition of the Lord's Prayer is the only petition with a condition attached to it: "As we also have forgiven our debtors [those who trespass against us]." Not too much should be made of the condition. Weighed in the balance against what is offered, it is next to nothing. But it serves to remind us that forgiveness is more than a feeling, a forgetting, a resolve not to take revenge. Forgiveness is a deed, an exchange of places, an affirmative action.

SESSION PLANS

Learning Objectives

This session is intended to enable participants to:

1. Outline the essential features of the Jubilee Year.

2. Interpret the conditional nature of forgiveness in Matthew 18:21-35.

3. Distinguish the relative advantages of using "debts," "trespasses," or "sins" in the Lord's Prayer.

Resources You May Need

Newsprint and markers or a chalkboard and chalk
A hymnbook

Leadership Strategy

SETTING THE STAGE

1. Lead the group in a prayer of confession and assurance of pardon from a Sunday liturgy in your congregation or a worship resource of your denomination.

2. Continue with your usual scheme for summarizing the previous session and eliciting questions about the reading assignment.

3. Ask participants to share with the group any previous associations they have with the concept of "Jubilee" or the "Jubilee Year." (There are African-American spirituals that draw on this concept. Sometimes the celebration of fifty years in the reign of a monarch or the life of an institution will be called a "Golden Jubilee.")

and/or

If participants have followed the suggestion of listing persons or institutions to whom they owe money or who owe money to them, invite them to comment on these lists. How do they feel about being in debt to someone? What emotional ties do they have to those who are in debt to them?

EXPLORING THE SCRIPTURE

1. Give a brief presentation on the Year of Jubilee or introduce the person who agreed to undertake this assignment at the last session. Commentaries on Leviticus and Bible dictionaries will be helpful sources of information.

and/or

Write on a chalkboard or separate sheets of newsprint three headings: Release, Redemption, Restoration. Divide the group into three subgroups and assign each subgroup one of the headings. The groups are to read Leviticus 25 and list the various provisions for the Year of Jubilee which fall under their heading. Indicate that some of the provisions may not fit under these headings and some may fit under more than one heading.

After ten or fifteen minutes reassemble the large group and have the subgroups present the results of their work. (You should be prepared to explain any provisions that are obscure. A commentary on Leviticus will be a useful resource.) Remind the group that Mr. Purdy says that forgiveness in the Bible includes release, restoration, and redemption. Ask how this study of Leviticus 25 illustrates or helps us to understand these three dimensions.

and

Test the group's comprehension of these concepts by analyzing the language of familiar hymns. "O Zion, Haste, Thy Mission High Fulfilling," has as its refrain, "Publish glad tidings, tidings of peace, tidings of Jesus, redemption, and release." Ask: What do redemption and release mean to the hymnwriter? To you?

"Crown Him with Many Crowns," includes the phrase, "All hail, Redeemer, hail! For thou hast died for me." Why do we call Jesus our Redeemer? What does a redeemer do?

"Hail to the Brightness of Zion's Glad Morning" hails "the millions from bondage returning." Why does the hymnwriter speak of a return? Who is coming back? From where? To what?

2. Ask one member of the group to read Matthew 18:21-35 aloud. Invite five other persons to mime the actions in the parable as it is being read. Have one person play the king, one the unforgiving servant, one the luckless fellow slave, and two the servants who report to the king the failure of the first servant to be forgiving. After the reading ask: What does the parable teach about the conditions and the process for receiving forgiveness?

and/or

Write on newsprint or a chalkboard the heading "The Steps in Forgiveness" and ask the group to use the parable in Matthew 18:21-35 to chart the course or progress of forgiveness. Who takes the first step? What is the second step? etc. Record the responses on the newsprint. Lead the group in discussing how these steps are related to the dimensions of release, restoration and redemption we discussed earlier.

3. Introduce the three members of the group selected at the last session to make brief presentations about alternate phrasings for the fifth petition of the Lord's Prayer. One person is to present the rationale for using "trespasses," another the reasons for saying "debts," and the third the advantages of referring to "sins." Commentaries on Matthew and Luke and directories for worship will provide helpful information.

Following the presentations, poll the group members for their opinions. What are their preferences? Why?

and/or

Invite participants to suggest endings for the following stories, which are variations on the theme of "The Parable of the Unforgiving Servant."

a. Once there was a great landowner who was well-known for his merciless dealings with poachers. Whenever a poacher was caught, the landowner had one of his thumbs cut off. Even the king's son was not spared. On a dare from his young friends, he tried his luck at poaching salmon, was caught, and lost a thumb! After some years, the landowner joined in a rebellion against a newly-crowned king. The rebellion failed, and he was seized. Before his head was cut off, he asked for an audience with the king. When he came into the monarch's presence, the king held out a hand that was missing a thumb and said to him:

b. Once Jesus came upon a crowd that was stoning a prostitute. Jesus interposed himself between the crowd and the woman and stopped the stoning. Looking around at the crowd he said sternly, "Let any of you who is without sin throw another stone." At this the crowd dispersed. "Go and sin no more," Jesus told the woman. Later that day he chanced upon the woman again. She had a younger woman by the hair and was demanding the repayment of a loan. Jesus got between the two and said to the older woman:

After discussing the endings suggested for the stories, write the words debts, trespasses, and sins on a chalkboard or newsprint. Lead the group in analyzing which endings fit most appropriately with each of the alternate terms for the fifth petition of the Lord's Prayer.

CLOSING

1. Invite the group members to assume the posture of prayer and ask them to imagine themselves in the following situation:

A recession has turned into a terrible depression. Millions have defaulted on their home mortgages, credit card payments, and college loans. Huge debtor camps have been created to hold these poor wretches who have no money, no credit, no way to pay for food and clothing. They have become wards of the government. In these camps are worthy citizens who simply lost their jobs and could not find work. Also in the camps are people who could not or would not do honest work: con artists, swindlers, hoboes, thieves, the aged, the infirm, persons with severe physical disabilities, drug dealers, and the like. Life in the camps is a desperate struggle for space, warmth, security, food, self-respect, and the attention of the authorities. You have been tossed into this camp because you could not meet your financial obligations. Daily you say your prayers, ending always with the Lord's Prayer.

Then lead the group in saying the Lord's Prayer.

or

If a member of the group has prepared a "scenario" for your closing prayer, invite that person to create the imaginary setting for your prayer.

or

For your closing prayer use the words of a hymn such as "Just As I Am, Without One Plea," or "Amazing Grace."

Looking Ahead

1. Mention that the next session is the last. Urge the group members to write down lingering questions they have about anything you have discussed to this point and to bring those to the next session.

2. In activity #2 under Exploring the Scripture, it is suggested that a member of the group present a minilecture on the various names and terms for evil. See the activity for details.

   An alternate suggestion in the same section is for two volunteers to present a brief debate on the question, "Does it make a difference whether there really is a devil?" Again, see the activity for details.

And do not bring us to the time of trial,
but rescue us from the evil one

CHAPTER SIX

Crying for Help

NOTES FROM THE AUTHOR

A man from California—elderly, to judge from his handwriting—sent this question to my column in a denominational magazine: "Why would God lead us into temptation ('... and lead us not into temptation,' Matthew 6:13)?"

I wrote back: "First, let me offer some alternative readings of Matthew 6:13: 'And do not bring us to the time of trial' (NRSV). 'And do not bring us to the test' (NEB). 'And do not put us to the test' (JB). 'Do not bring us to hard testing' (TEV). What these various readings bring to mind are not temptations in the usual sense. Rather they bring to mind Jesus' testing in the wilderness. He was led or driven there by God's own Spirit, and there he wrestled with the temptations to become a popular hero, to cooperate with the ruling systems, and to put God's promises to the test. If God were to put us to the tests that Jesus faced, we would fail miserably. Therefore, knowing our weaknesses, we ask in the Lord's Prayer that we not be led into places where such testing takes place. However, if we should be so led and so tested, we also pray, 'But deliver us from evil' (or 'the evil one'). Should events transpire that confront us with terror or torture, we pray that God will in that hour deliver us."

Just as the fifth petition challenges us with a complexity of terms, debts/trespasses/sins, so the sixth petition challenges us with trial/test/temptation and evil/evil one. By setting the petition in the context of Jesus' forty days in the wilderness, I have tried to show that it is not a case of either/or but rather both/and. And by linking the petition to Israel's history, I have tried to show that certain events or eras are times of testing for all of God's people. We should not be misled by Jesus' lonely wilderness experience to think of temptation as happening to individuals in isolation from society.

And so we pray lead **us** not into the time of trial, but rescue **us** from the evil one. The sixth petition is deeply personal. We cannot escape involvement in or responsibility for the evil times that try us to the limit. All of which underscores the opening assertion of Chapter Six of the *Resource Book*, namely that prayer is a cry, a shriek, a moan.

SESSION PLANS

Learning Objectives

This session is intended to enable participants to:

1. Use Psalm 106 to trace the zigzag course of Israel between obedience and rebellion.

2. Summarize Jesus' temptations and suggest a contemporary parallel for each.

3. Describe the advantages of the version of the sixth petition of the Lord's Prayer they prefer.

Resources You May Need

Newsprint and markers or a chalkboard and chalk
Materials and supplies for the closing you design

Leadership Strategy

SETTING THE STAGE

1. Lead the group in an opening prayer. Then, if members of the group have brought written questions, ask that they be handed to you. Read them aloud. Ask for volunteers to offer responses. Give your own brief responses to questions that the group will not tackle. Be up front about admitting inability to respond to difficult or ambiguous questions. But try in one way or another to respond to each query. When you honor questions in this way, you encourage adults to continue to ask questions, and that is how they will continue to learn.

2. This last session of the study takes up one of the most intriguing and difficult petitions. Look back and get an overview of where you have been. But don't slight the subject matter.

Here is one way you might combine the two concerns: Ask for reactions of participants to the answer given to the woman from Washington who wrote to the author to ask, "Who rules this world—God or Satan?" (See page 62 of the *Resource Book*.) The answer includes a quick overview of the entire Lord's Prayer. Ask one person to read aloud the woman's question and another to read the author's response. Ask: What questions are raised by this interchange that we ought to try to answer in this final session?

or

Offer your own summary of the sessions to date. The author's comments in the section of the *Resource Book* titled "Biblical Spirituality" will provide a framework for your remarks. You may want to list on newsprint or a chalkboard the various dichotomies he describes (self-actualization/self-effacement, optimism/pessimism, etc.)

EXPLORING THE SCRIPTURE

1. Invite participants to open their Bibles to Psalm 106. On newsprint or a chalkboard draw a zigzag line representing high points and low points. Label it: "High Moments and Hard Times." Ask the group to read quickly through Psalm 106, noting as high points for your graph the great works of God on behalf of Israel, and as low points examples of Israel's failure to be obedient. Here are some points to be included:

High Points	Low Points
Red Sea rescue	Rebellion at Red Sea
Exodus from Egypt	God tested at Meribah
Covenant at Sinai (Horeb)	Jealousy of Moses, Aaron
Promised Land	Golden Calf worshiped
Many deliverances	Grumbling and disobedience
	Idolatry
	Mingling with the nations

Ask participants: If you were asked to grade the performance of Israel on a scale of 0 to 10, with 10 being "excellent," where would you put them? Encourage members of the group to give reasons for their choices.

and/or

Refer to the description of "hard times" on pages 58-59 in the *Resource Book*. Ask: Which of the failures of Israel recounted in Psalm 106 might be described as flunking the test of hard times? When in the history of the church have we responded to hard times in less than praiseworthy ways? In what ways do members of the group think that we are currently failing some critical tests of will and purpose as a community of faith?

2. Remind the group of the Gospel story about Jesus being put to critical tests. Ask members to turn in their Bibles to Matthew 4:1-11. Note first of all any parts of the narrative that are related to what has been discussed in previous sessions. For example, there is a direct quote from Deuteronomy 8. There is also a reference to bread. Point out that the reference to putting God to the test has to do with the incident at Meribah, already noted in this session in the review of Psalm 106.

and

Divide the group into three smaller groups and assign each small group one of Jesus' temptations. They are to review the biblical material in Matthew 4:1-11 and the comments on pages 59-61 of the *Resource Book*.

The assignment is to summarize the significance of the temptation for Jesus and to recast that temptation into contemporary terms. What might it mean today to turn stones into bread, to test God's promises, to grasp for worldwide power? Each group should select one person to report its work to the others when the whole group is reconvened.

and/or

Present a minilecture on the various names and terms for evil (the devil, Satan, the evil one, etc.) or introduce the person who volunteered for this assignment at the last session. A Bible dictionary, such as *Harpers*, will provide helpful background information.

Then lead the group in discussing its understanding of temptation, using questions such as the following:

a. To what extent do you believe the personification of evil is warranted? Helpful?

b. When your faith is tested, how often do you attribute this temptation to an evil force or person?

c. How does your understanding of evil enable you to acknowledge the persistence or permissiveness of temptation? How does it encourage you to trust in God? To take responsibility for your life?

Introduce the two volunteers who agreed to present a debate on the question, "Does it make a difference whether there really is a devil?" Each person should have 3-5 minutes to make a statement and a one-minute follow-up speech. Bible dictionaries, church confessions, statements of faith and theology texts will be useful for preparation. You might also want to note Mr. Purdy's position in the sections in the *Resource Book* entitled "Biblical Spirituality" and "Who Rules the World?"

Following the debate, invite the group to respond to the issues raised by the presenters or lead a discussion using the questions listed above.

3. Write on newsprint or a chalkboard variant readings of the sixth petition of the Lord's Prayer.

"And do not bring us to the time of trial, but deliver us from the evil one." (NRSV)

"Do not bring us to hard testing but keep us safe from the Evil One." (TEV)

"And do not put us to the test, but save us from the evil one." (Jerusalem Bible)

If participants have other variations of Matthew 6:13 in the Bibles they prefer, list those as well.

Then lead the group members through a process in which they declare their preference for the language of the sixth petition. Discover, by a show of hands, how many prefer each choice. Invite several persons from each preference group to share their opinions.

CLOSING

1. Allow at least ten minutes at the end of your time together for the group to come to some kind of closure on the experience. A casual "See you around" is not very satisfying, nor does it invite persons to continue their learning. Each leader will have a preference for closing activities. Some leaders make an elaborate ceremony out of closure: They present small gifts or tokens of the experience—a book, a plaque, a pin, a card. Other leaders prefer a time of personal sharing, in which each participant has a last chance to share an insight or an abiding question. Still others think some kind of brief service of worship is most

appropriate, with a worship center or focus (a lighted candle, a picture, a chalice), Scripture, prayer, a hymn.

Plan a closing that seems right for you and your group, something that indicates to everyone that you—the leader—have learned much, have been challenged, have appreciated the presence of every person attending.

and

Ask participants to form a friendship circle, and with hands held, say the Lord's Prayer together one last time.

APPENDIX

Guidelines for Adult Education

The following guidelines provide a summary of the most recent findings about adult education.

- **Adults are responsible for their own learning.**

  Therefore, it is important not to develop dependent relationships whereby the learners look to the leader as the authority and primary source of information.

- **Adults learn best when they can participate directly in the process of their own learning.**

  Therefore, opportunities should be provided in each session for participants to make decisions about what and how they will learn and to interact with the subject matter and other learners.

- **Adults represent a variety of learning styles as well as different stages of physical, emotional and spiritual development.**

  Therefore, learners will be related to individually without assuming that all adults are the same. Learners will be encouraged to work at their own pace and to make applications that are appropriate to themselves.

- **Learning is reinforced best when adults have the opportunity to practice skills and to express ideas in their own words.**

  Therefore, in each session there will be opportunities to practice particular skills and to express personal insights and interpretation.

51

- **Learning occurs within an environment of trusting relationships.**

  Therefore, it is important to develop a process whereby persons will be encouraged to share feelings, needs, and concerns as well as information and ideas. In such a setting persons will be helped to become caring about and supportive of one another.

- **With adults it is not necessary to use competitive activities to motivate them to want to participate and learn.**

  Therefore, the activities and resources will represent a cooperative, collaborative style of learning.

- **Adults who have positive self-concepts are less threatened by new information and experiences.**

  Therefore, leaders will be encouraged to use strategies that enhance a person's sense of self-worth.

- **Adults will increase their knowledge and skill to a greater extent when they gain a sense of satisfaction and experience success in those activities that are planned for them.**

  Therefore, the session plans of the Kerygma Program study resources will present a variety of activities that are designed to enable participants to achieve satisfaction and success.

— Notes —

— Notes —

NOTES

NOTES